A New Way
of *Thinking,*

A New Way
of *Being*

A New Way
of *Thinking,*
A New Way
of *Being*

Experiencing the Tao Te Ching

Dr. Wayne W. Dyer

LIFE
Styles

HAY HOUSE, INC.
Carlsbad, California • New York City
London • Sydney • Johannesburg
Vancouver • Hong Kong • New Delhi

Published and distributed in the United States by: Hay House, Inc.:
www.hayhouse.com • *Published and distributed in Australia by:*
Hay House Australia Pty. Ltd.: www.hayhouse.com.au • *Published
and distributed in the United Kingdom by:* Hay House UK, Ltd.:
www.hayhouse.co.uk • *Published and distributed in the Republic
of South Africa by:* Hay House SA (Pty), Ltd.: www.hayhouse
.co.za • *Distributed in Canada by:* Raincoast: www.raincoast
.com • *Published in India by:* Hay House Publishers India: www
.hayhouse.co.in

Editorial supervision: Jill Kramer   *Design:* Nick Welch

The material in this book was adapted from the book *Change Your
Thoughts—Change Your Life* (Hay House, Inc., 2007), as well as the
Change Your Thoughts—Change Your Life Perpetual Flip Calendar, by
Dr. Wayne W. Dyer (Hay House, Inc., 2008).

Library of Congress Control Number: 2007938124

ISBN: 978-1-4019-2151-4

13 12 11 10   4 3 2 1
1st edition, July 2010

Printed in China

Introduction

This beautiful book offers you an opportunity to internalize and directly experience the great wisdom of the Tao Te Ching, a collection of 81 verses authored by Chinese prophet Lao-tzu 25 centuries ago.

The words *Tao Te Ching* translate to "living and applying the Great Way." The Tao is considered by many scholars to be the wisest book ever written, and it encourages you to change your life by literally changing the way you think.

Within these pages, I've broken down the translated verses* that appear in full in my book *Change Your Thoughts— Change Your Life* into bite-size pieces—and edited and rearranged them as needed for sense and clarity—so that you can slowly absorb these powerful thoughts and imprint them into your consciousness.

Working with one concept at a time, you will come to know the truth behind the ancient Tao observation: *When you change the way you look at things, the things you look at change.*

— Dr. Wayne W. Dyer

*Please note: Some versions of the Tao I relied upon more than others, and I would like to especially mention that the version provided by Jonathan Star (in *Tao Te Ching: the Definitive Edition*) was the one I quoted most extensively and the one that most resonated with my vision and interpretation of the Tao. (In particular, major portions of verses 6, 13, 18, 29, 30, 33, 38, 39, 44, 46, 49, 54, 56, 58, 62, 67, 69, 72, 74, 76, and 79 in *Change Your Thoughts—Change Your Life* were quoted from Star's translation.)

I would recommend that anyone seeking to gain a greater insight into the verses of the Tao Te Ching—something that could deepen one's understanding of the ideas provided in this book—should consult Jonathan Star's version. His edition of the Tao Te Ching is unique in that it not only provides an elegant translation of the verses, but also provides a word-for-word translation of every Chinese character found in the original text. By use of this verbatim translation, even those who do not know ancient Chinese can gain significant insight into the meaning of the original work.

*The Tao is both
named and nameless.
As nameless it is the
origin of all things;
as named it is the
Mother of 10,000 things.*

The Tao that can be told
is not the eternal Tao.
The name that can be named
is not the eternal name.

Ever desireless, one can

see the mystery.

Ever desiring, one sees only

the manifestations.

The mystery itself is the doorway

to all understanding.

Under heaven all can

see beauty as beauty

only because there is ugliness.

All can know good as good

only because there is evil.

Being and nonbeing

produce each other.

The difficult is born in the easy.

Long is defined by short,

the high by the low.

Before and after go along

with each other.

*The sage can act
without effort
and teach
without words.*

When the work
of the Tao is done,
it is forgotten.
That is why
it lasts forever.

Putting a value

on status creates

contentiousness.

The sage governs
by emptying minds
and hearts,
by weakening
ambitions and
strengthening bones.

Practice not doing. . . .
When action is
pure and selfless,
everything settles
into its own
perfect place.

The Tao is empty

but inexhaustible,

bottomless, the

ancestor of all.

Within the Tao,

the sharp edges

become smooth;

the twisted

knots loosen.

The Tao is hidden

but always present.

It is not known who

gave birth to it.

Heaven and earth
are impartial;
they see the 10,000 things
as straw dogs.
The sage is not sentimental;
he treats all his people
as straw dogs.

The sage is like

heaven and earth:

To him none are

especially dear,

nor is there anyone

he disfavors.

*The sage gives
and gives,
without condition,
offering his treasures
to everyone.*

*Between heaven and
earth is a space like
a bellows; empty and
inexhaustible, the more
it is used, the more
it produces.*

Hold on to your center.
Man was made
to sit quietly
and find the
truth within.

The spirit that

never dies is called

the mysterious feminine.

Although she becomes

the whole universe,

her immaculate purity

is never lost.

Although the mysterious feminine assumes countless forms, her true identity remains intact.

The gateway to the mysterious

feminine is called

the root of creation.

Listen to her voice,

hear it echo

through creation.

Without fail,
the mysterious feminine
reveals her presence.
Without fail,
she brings us to our
own perfection.

Heaven is eternal—
the earth endures.
Why do heaven and
earth last forever?
They do not live for
themselves only.
This is the secret of
their durability.

The sage puts

himself last

and so ends

up ahead.

*Serve the needs
of others, and all
your own needs
will be fulfilled.*

*Through selfless
action,
fulfillment is
attained.*

The supreme good
is like water,
which nourishes all
things without
trying to.

*Live in accordance
with the nature of things.
This is the Tao.*

In dealing with others,
be gentle and kind.
Stand by your word.

One who lives

in accordance with nature

does not go against

the way of things.

To keep on filling
is not as good as stopping.
Overfilled, the cupped
hands drip,
better to stop pouring.

Sharpen a blade
too much and its edge
will soon be lost.
Fill your house with
jade and gold and
it brings insecurity.

Retire when the

work is done;

this is the way

of heaven.

*Carrying body
and soul and
embracing the one,
can you avoid separation?*

Can you let your

body become as supple

as a newborn child's?

In the opening and shutting

of heaven's gate, can you play

the feminine part?

Can you love your

people and govern

your domain

without

self-importance?

Giving birth
and nourishing;
having, yet not
possessing . . .
this is the Tao.

Thirty spokes converge

upon a single hub;

it is on the hole

in the center that

the use of the

cart hinges.

Shape clay into a vessel;

it is the space within

that makes it useful.

Carve fine doors and windows,

but the room is useful

in its emptiness.

The usefulness

of what is

depends on

what is not.

The five colors blind the eye. The five tones deafen the ear. The five flavors dull the taste. The chase and the hunt craze people's minds.

Wasting energy

to obtain rare objects

only impedes

one's growth.

The master

observes the world

but trusts his

inner vision.

Seeking favor
is degrading: alarming
when it is gotten,
alarming when it is lost.

The reason we have

a lot of trouble

is that we have selves.

If we had no selves,

what trouble

would we have?

Man's true self

is eternal, yet he thinks,

I am this body and

will soon die.

If we have no body,

what calamities

can we have?

*One who sees
himself as everything
is fit to be guardian
of the world.*

That which cannot
be seen is called invisible.
That which cannot be heard
is called inaudible.
That which cannot be held
is called intangible.
These three cannot
be defined; therefore,
they are merged as one.

Discovering how things

have always been

brings one into

harmony with

the Way.

The ancient masters

were profound

and subtle.

Their wisdom was

unfathomable.

*Open yourself to
the Tao and trust your
natural responses . . .
then everything will
fall into place.*

The muddiest

water clears

as it is stilled.

And out of that

stillness,

life arises.

He who keeps the Tao

does not want to be full.

But precisely because

he is never full,

he can remain like

a hidden sprout

and does not rush

to early ripening.

Become totally empty.

Let your heart

be at peace.

Amidst the rush of worldly comings and goings, observe how endings become beginnings.

Things flourish,

each by each,

only to return

to the Source . . .

to what is and

what is to be.

To return to the root

is to find peace.

To find peace is to fulfill

one's destiny.

Knowing the constant
gives perspective.
This perspective is impartial.
Impartiality is the
highest nobility.
The highest nobility
is Divine.

Being Divine, you will

be at one with the Tao.

Being at one with the

Tao is eternal.

With the greatest

leader above them,

people barely know

one exists.

*The pieces of a chariot
are useless unless they work in
accordance with the whole.
A man's life brings nothing
unless he lives in accordance
with the whole universe.*

When the greatness of the Tao

is present, action arises

from one's own heart.

When the greatness of the Tao

is absent, action comes

from the rules of

"kindness and justice."

If you need rules to be

kind and just,

if you <u>act</u> virtuous,

this is a sure sign

that virtue is absent.

Thus we see the

great hypocrisy.

When kinship falls

into discord, piety and rites

of devotion arise. When a

country falls into chaos,

official loyalists will appear;

patriotism is born.

Give up sainthood,

renounce wisdom,

and it will be a hundred

times better for everyone.

*Throw away
morality and justice
and people will do
the right thing.*

A contented man
is never disappointed.
He who knows when
to stop is preserved from
peril, only thus can
you endure long.

*It is more important
to see the simplicity,
to realize one's true nature,
to cast off selfishness
and temper desire.*

Give up learning and you

will be free from all your cares.

What is the difference

between yes and no?

What is the difference

between good and evil?

Must you fear

what others fear?

Should you fear

desolation when there

is abundance?

You are but a guest

in this world.

While others rush about

to get things done,

you accept what is offered.

Drift like a wave

on the ocean.

Blow as aimless

as the wind.

The greatest virtue is to follow the Tao and the Tao alone.

*Although formless
and intangible,
the Tao gives rise to form.
Although vague and elusive,
it gives rise to shapes.*

Throughout the ages,

the Tao's name

has been preserved

in order to recall the

beginning of all things.

The old saying

that the flexible are

preserved unbroken

is surely right!

If you have truly

attained wholeness,

everything will

flock to you.

The sage doesn't

display himself,

so people can

see his light.

The Tao is hidden

and nameless;

the Tao alone

nourishes and

brings everything

to fulfillment.

To truly see the Tao,

see it as it is. In a person,

see it as a person; in a family,

see it as a family; in a country,

see it as a country; in the world,

see it as the world.

An army that cannot
yield will be defeated.
A tree that cannot bend
will crack in the wind.

To talk little is natural:

Fierce winds do not

blow all morning;

a downpour of rain does

not last the day.

*If heaven and
earth cannot sustain
a forced action,
how much less
is man able to do?*

*Those who follow
the Way become one
with the Way.*

These teachings are very
easy to understand
and very easy to practice;
yet so few in this world
understand, and so
few are able to practice.

*Those who stray from
the Way and goodness
become one with failure.*

*If you conform
to the Way, its power
flows through you.*

The ancient masters

were watchful, like men

crossing a winter stream.

Alert, like men aware of danger.

Simple as uncarved wood.

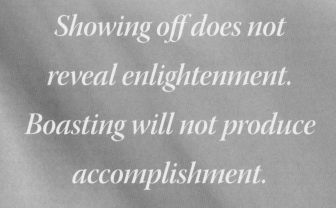

Showing off does not reveal enlightenment. Boasting will not produce accomplishment.

Nobility is rooted in humility;

loftiness is based on lowliness.

This is why noble people

refer to themselves as alone,

lacking, and unworthy.

Just as all water flows back

to become the ocean,

all creation flows back to

become the Tao.

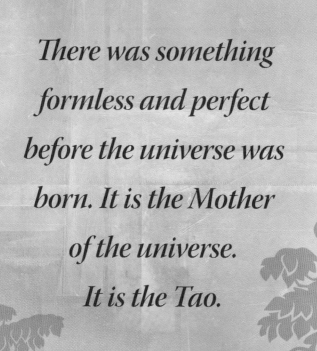

*There was something
formless and perfect
before the universe was
born. It is the Mother
of the universe.
It is the Tao.*

The Way is great,

heaven is great,

earth is great,

people are great.

To know humanity,

understand earth.

To know earth,

understand heaven.

The heavy is the root of the light. The still is the master of unrest.

The successful person is poised and centered in the midst of all activities.

If you let yourself
be blown to and fro,
you lose touch with your
root. To be restless is to lose
one's self-mastery.

A knower of the truth

travels without leaving

a trace, speaks without

causing harm, gives without

keeping an account.

*Be wise and help
all beings impartially,
abandoning none.*

Waste no opportunities. This is called following the light.

What is a good man

but a bad man's teacher?

What is a bad man

but a good man's job?

If the teacher
is not respected and
the student not cared for,
confusion will arise,
however clever one is.
This is the great secret.

Know the strength
of man, but keep
a woman's care!

To be the pattern

of the world is to move

constantly in the path of virtue

without erring a single step,

and to return again

to the infinite.

One who understands
splendor while holding
to humility acts in accord
with eternal power.

To be the fountain
of the world is to live
the abundant life
of virtue.

When the unformed
is formed into objects,
its original qualities
are lost.

Do you think you

can take over

the universe and

improve it?

It cannot

be done.

Everything under heaven is a sacred vessel and cannot be controlled. Trying to control leads to ruin. Trying to grasp, you lose.

*Allow your life
to unfold naturally.
Know that it is
a vessel of
perfection.*

There is a time for being
ahead and a time for being
behind; a time for being
in motion and a time
for being at rest.

To the sage,

all of life is a movement

toward perfection,

so what need has

he for the excessive,

the extravagant,

or the extreme?

One who would guide

a leader of men in the uses

of life will warn him against

the use of arms for conquest.

Weapons often turn

upon the wielder.

Where armies settle,

nature offers nothing but briars

and thorns. After a great battle

has been fought, the land

is cursed, the crops fail,

the earth lies stripped

of its Motherhood.

*After you have attained
your purpose, you must
not parade your success,
you must not boast
of your ability, you must
not feel proud.*

The highest virtue is to act
without a sense of self.
The highest kindness is to give
without condition.
The highest justice is to see
without preference.

Whatever strains with force will soon decay. It is not attuned to the Way. Not being attuned to the Way, its end comes all too soon.

Weapons are the

tools of violence;

all decent men detest them.

Therefore, followers of

the Tao never use them.

Take on difficulties
while they are still easy;
do great things
while they are
still small.

Peace and quiet
are dearest to the
decent man's heart,
and to him even a victory
is no cause for rejoicing.

He who thinks

triumph beautiful

is one with a will to kill,

and one with a will to kill

shall never prevail

upon the world.

It is a good sign
when man's higher nature
comes forward, a bad sign
when his lower nature
comes forward.

With the slaughter
of multitudes, we have
grief and sorrow. Every
victory is a funeral;
when you win a war,
you celebrate
by mourning.

The eternal Tao
has no name. Although
simple and subtle, no one
in the world can master it.

Once the whole is divided,

the parts need names.

There are already enough

names; know when

to stop. Know when

reason sets limits

to avoid peril.

*Rivers and streams
are born of the ocean,
and all creation is
born of the Tao.*

One who understands

others has knowledge;

one who understands

himself has wisdom.

*Mastering others
requires force; mastering
the self needs strength.*

If you realize that
you have enough,
you are truly rich.

One who gives himself

to his position surely lives

long. One who gives

himself to the Tao

surely lives forever.

The Great Way is universal;

it can apply to the left or the

right. All beings depend on

it for life; even so, it does not

take possession of them.

All things, including the grass and trees, are soft and pliable in life; dry and brittle in death.

Cultivated in the self, virtue is realized; cultivated in the family, virtue overflows; cultivated in the community, virtue increases; cultivated in the state, virtue abounds.

*By not claiming
greatness,
the sage achieves
greatness.*

Music and dining are

passing pleasures,

yet they cause people to stop.

How bland and insipid are

the things of this world

when one compares

them to the Tao!

When you look for the Tao,
there is nothing to see.
When you listen for it,
there is nothing to hear.

Should you want
to contain something,
you must deliberately
let it expand.

The Tao is not something

found at the marketplace

or passed on from father

to son. It is not something

gained by knowing

or lost by forgetting.

Those who have virtue

do not look for faults;

those who look for faults

have no virtue.

Be content with healthy
food, pleased with
useful clothing,
satisfied in snug homes,
and protective of your
way of life.

*The gentle outlasts
the strong. The obscure
outlasts the obvious.*

Fish cannot leave deep

waters, and a country's

weapons should not

be displayed.

The Tao does nothing, but leaves nothing undone.

*Because the sage
has no goal in mind,
everything he
does succeeds.*

When life is simple,
pretenses fall away;
our essential natures
shine through.

*By not wanting,
there is calm, and the world
will straighten itself.*

When there is silence,
one finds the anchor of the
universe within oneself.

A truly good man is not aware of his goodness and is therefore good. A foolish man tries to be good and is therefore not good.

The master does nothing,

yet he leaves nothing undone.

The ordinary man is

always doing things,

yet many more are

left to be done.

You must never think

of conquering others

by force.

When the Tao is lost,

there is goodness.

When goodness is lost,

there is morality.

When morality is lost,

there is ritual.

Ritual is the husk of true faith,

the beginning of chaos.

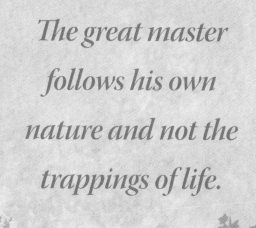

The great master
follows his own
nature and not the
trappings of life.

It is said:

"The great master stays with the

fruit and not the fluff.

He stays with the firm

and not the flimsy.

He stays with the true

and not the false."

The master acts

without expectation

and succeeds without

taking credit.

When man interferes
with the Tao,
the sky becomes filthy,
the earth becomes depleted,
the equilibrium crumbles, and
creatures become extinct.

He who is self-righteous

is not respected.

He who boasts

will not endure.

*A great leader speaks
little. He never
speaks carelessly.*

Playing one's part

in accordance with

the universe

is true humility.

Too much honor

means no honor.

It is not wise to

shine like jade

and resound like

stone chimes.

The Tao gave birth to one.

One gave birth to two.

Two gave birth to three.

And three begat the

10,000 things.

The 10,000 things carry yin

and embrace yang;

they achieve harmony by

combining these forces.

Nothing in the world is softer

and weaker than water.

But for attacking the

hard, the unyielding,

nothing can surpass it.

There is nothing like it.

A great scholar hears
of the Tao and begins
diligent practice.
A middling scholar
hears of the Tao
and retains some
and loses some.

That without

substance

enters where

there is no space.

Hence, the value

of nonaction.

Because the sage has

nothing to prove,

people can trust

his words.

*One gains
by losing,
and loses
by gaining.*

*The violent do not
die a natural death.
That is a
fundamental
teaching.*

The softest of all things

overrides the hardest

of all things.

Teaching without words, performing without actions—few in the world can grasp it—that is the master's way.

*Rare indeed are
those who obtain the
bounty of this world.*

Which means more to you,

you or your renown?

Which brings more to you,

you or what you own?

What you gain

is more trouble

than what you lose.

Love is the
fruit of sacrifice.
Wealth is the fruit
of generosity.

*Throw away
industry and profit
and there will be
no thieves.*

The greatest perfection
seems imperfect,
and yet its use is inexhaustible.
The greatest fullness
seems empty, and yet
its use is endless.

Great straightness
seems twisted. Great
intelligence seems stupid.
Great eloquence
seems awkward.
Great truth seems false.
Great discussion
seems silent.

Activity conquers cold;
inactivity conquers heat.
Stillness and tranquility
set things in order
in the universe.

When the world has the

Way, running horses are

retired to till the fields.

When the world lacks the Way,

warhorses are bred

in the countryside.

There is no greater loss

than losing the Tao,

no greater curse

than covetousness,

no greater tragedy

than discontentment.

The worst of
faults is
wanting more—
always.

*Contentment alone
is enough. Indeed, the bliss
of eternity can be found
in your contentment.*

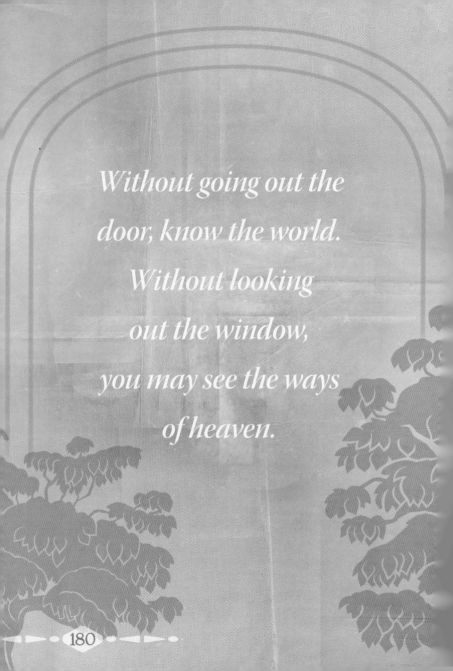

*Without going out the
door, know the world.
Without looking
out the window,
you may see the ways
of heaven.*

The farther

one goes,

the less

one knows.

The sage does not
venture forth
and yet knows, does not
look and yet names.

*Learning consists
of daily accumulating.
The practice of the Tao
consists of daily
diminishing; decreasing
and decreasing,
until doing nothing.*

When nothing

is done,

nothing is

left undone.

*True mastery can
be gained by letting things
go their own way.*

The sage has
no fixed mind;
he is aware of the
needs of others.

Those who are good

the sage treats with

goodness. Those who are bad

he also treats with goodness,

because the nature

of his being is good.

Heaven does not ask,
yet it is supplied with
all that it needs.

The sage knows

himself but makes

no show of himself.

Governing a large country
is like frying a small fish.
You spoil it with
too much poking.

Open your mouth,

always be busy,

and life is

beyond hope.

Seeing the small is called clarity; keeping flexible is called strength.

Realize your essence
and you will witness the
end without ending.

The Way connects all

living beings to their Source.

It springs into existence,

unconscious, perfect, free.

All beings honor the Way

and value its virtue.

They have not been commanded

to worship the Tao

and do homage to virtue,

but they do so spontaneously.

The Tao gives all beings life.

Virtue nourishes and

nurtures them,

rears and shelters and

protects them.

The Tao produces but does not possess; it gives without expecting.

The Tao fosters

growth without

ruling. This is called

hidden virtue.

All under heaven have

a common beginning.

This beginning is the

Mother of the world.

Keep your mouth shut,

guard the senses,

and life is ever full.

Using the shining radiance,
you return again to the
light and save yourself
misfortune. This is called
the practice of eternal light.

Pomp at the
expense of others
is like the boasting of
thieves after a looting.
This is not the Tao.

The net of heaven

catches all;

its mesh is coarse,

but nothing

slips through.

If you are not afraid
of dying, there is nothing
you cannot achieve.

*Because the sage
doesn't know who he is,
people recognize
themselves in him.*

The Tao is everywhere;

it has become everything.

He who is in harmony

with the Tao

is like a newborn child.

Deadly insects

will not sting him.

Wild beasts will not attack him.

Birds of prey will not strike him.

*To know harmony is
to know the changeless;
to know the changeless
is to have insight.*

*Things in harmony
with the Tao remain;
things that are forced
grow for a while
but then wither away.
This is not the Tao.*

Whatever is against

the Tao soon ceases to be.

Those who know
do not talk.
Those who talk
do not know.

Close your mouth,

cordon off your senses,

blunt your sharpness,

untie your knots,

soften your glare,

settle your dust.

This is primal union or

the secret embrace.

If you want to be

a great leader,

you must learn

to follow the Tao.

Stop trying to control.
Let go of fixed plans
and concepts and the world
will govern itself.

In this world,

the greater the

restrictions and

prohibitions,

the more people are

impoverished.

The sage says:

"I take no action and

people are reformed.

I enjoy peace and

people become honest.

I do nothing and

people become rich."

When the ruler

knows his own heart,

the people are simple

and pure. When he

meddles with their lives,

they become restless

and disturbed.

*Bad fortune is what
good fortune leans on;
good fortune is what
bad fortune hides in.*

The master is

content to serve as

an example and not

to impose his will.

Should you want to take something away, you must deliberately grant it access.

*In governing people
and serving nature,
nothing surpasses thrift
and moderation.*

Restraint begins with giving up one's own ideas. This depends on virtue gathered in the past.

If nothing is impossible,
then there are no limits.
If a man knows no limits,
he is fit to lead.

The sage lives

in harmony with all

below heaven.

Approach

the universe

with the Tao

and evil will

have no power.

If a ruler and his people

would refrain from

harming each other,

all the benefits of life

would accumulate

in the kingdom.

A great country is
like the lowland
toward which all streams
flow. It is the reservoir
of all under heaven,
the feminine of the world.

If a great country lowers

itself before a small one,

it wins friendship and trust.

And if a small country can

lower itself before a great one,

it will win over that "great"

country. The one wins

by stooping; the other,

by remaining low.

*The Tao is the treasure-
house, the true nature,
the secret source
of everything.*

If a person seems wicked,

do not cast him away.

Awaken him with your

words, and elevate

him with your deeds.

When a new leader is chosen,

do not offer to help him

with your wealth or

your expertise.

Offer instead to teach

him about the Tao.

The Tao is the source

of all good

and the remedy

for all evil.

Practice nonaction.

Work without doing.

Taste the tasteless.

Magnify the small,

increase the few.

Reward bitterness

with care.

See simplicity in the complicated. Achieve greatness in little things.

Arms serve evil.
They are the tools of
those who oppose wise rule.
Use them only
as a last resort.

The sage does not attempt anything very big, and thus achieves greatness.

The Great Way accomplishes

its purpose but makes no

claim for itself. It covers

all creatures like the sky

but does not dominate them.

What is at rest is

easily managed.

What is not yet manifest

is easy to prevent.

Act before things exist;
manage them before
there is disorder.

True words often

appear paradoxical.

The sage does not act,
and so is not defeated.
He does not grasp and
therefore does not lose.

People usually fail
when they are
on the verge of success.
So give as much care at the
end as at the beginning,
and then there will be no failure.

The sage does not collect precious things; he learns not to hold on to ideas.

When they think that they

know the answers,

people are difficult to guide.

When they know they

do not know, people can

find their own way.

Not using cunning to govern a country is good fortune for the country.

The simplest pattern
is the clearest. Content with
an ordinary life, you can
show all people the way
back to their own true nature.

Why is the sea the king of
a hundred streams?
Because it lies below them.
Humility gives it its power.

The sage is kind

to the kind. He is also kind

to the unkind because

the nature of his being

is kindness.

The Great Way is very

smooth and straight,

yet the people prefer

devious paths.

The sage stays low
so the world never tires
of exalting him.

*Bold action against
others leads to death.
Bold action in
harmony with
the Tao leads to life.*

Should you want

to weaken something,

you must deliberately

let it grow strong.

Mercy, frugality,
and humility
are three treasures
to hold fast and
watch closely.

A great leader works

without self-interest

and leaves no trace.

When all is finished,

the people say,

"We did it ourselves."

The sage is faithful
to the faithful;
he is also faithful
to the unfaithful.

Love vanquishes
all attackers;
it is impregnable
in defense.

When heaven wants
to protect someone,
does it send an army?
No, it protects with love.

A good soldier

is not violent.

A good fighter

is not angry.

Good employers

serve their workers.

The best leader follows

the will of the people.

Noncompetition,

noncontending,

and employing the

powers of others

are virtues that form

the ultimate unity

with heaven.

There is a saying among

soldiers: "I dare not make

the first move but would

rather play the guest;

I dare not advance

an inch but would rather

withdraw a foot."

*There is no greater
misfortune than the
feeling "I have an enemy";
for when "I" and "enemy"
exist together, there is
no room left for the Tao.*

*When two opponents
meet, the one
without an enemy
will surely triumph.*

*When armies are
evenly matched, the one
with compassion wins.*

The sage dresses
plainly even though
his interior is filled
with precious gems.

Those who follow goodness become one with goodness.

Knowing ignorance

is strength.

Ignoring knowledge

is sickness.

When people lack a sense

of awe, there will be disaster.

When people do not fear

worldly power, a greater

power will arrive.

*The sage is
not sick but is sick
of sickness;
this is the secret
of health.*

Repay the seemingly wicked man with your kindness.

*Do not limit
the view of yourself.
Do not despise the
conditions of your birth.*

Nurturing things
without possessing
them, the sage works, but
not for rewards; he competes,
but not for results.

If one were bold

but had no mercy, if one

were broad but were not

frugal, if one went ahead

without humility . . .

one would die.

Because the master

has given up helping, he is

people's greatest help.

The sage remains

a servant

so the world never

tires of making

him its king.

It is heaven's way
to conquer without striving.
It does not speak,
yet it is answered.

Those desiring a position above others must speak humbly. Those desiring to lead must follow.

Whoever is planted

in the Tao will

not be rooted up.

Whoever embraces

the Tao will

not slip away.

If you realize that all things change, there is nothing you will try to hold on to.

All things return to the
Great Way as to their home,
but it does not lord it over
them; thus, it may
be called "great."

Whoever cuts
with the blade of
a master carpenter
is sure to cut
his own hands.

When taxes are

too high, people

go hungry.

When the government

is too intrusive,

people lose their spirit.

*Puff yourself
with honor and pride
and no one can
save you from a fall.*

The sage

always confronts

difficulties;

he never

experiences

them.

*Stiffness is
a companion
of death; flexibility
a companion
of life.*

If powerful men

could center themselves

in the Tao, the whole

world would be

transformed

by itself, in its

natural rhythms.

The hard and
stiff will be broken;
the soft and supple
will prevail.

The way of heaven
is like drawing a bow:
The high is lowered,
the low is raised.

The Tao reduces

deficiency in

order to add to

the surplus. It strips

the needy to serve

those who have

too much.

What man has more than enough and gives it to the world? Only the man of the Tao.

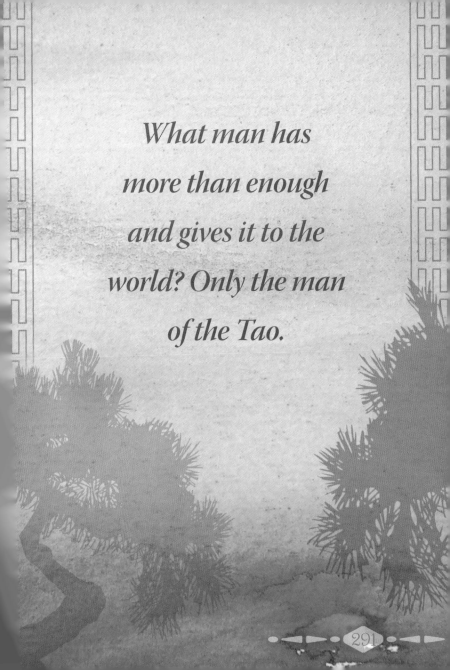

The master can
keep giving because
there is no end
to his wealth.

These things from ancient times arise from one: The sky is whole and clear. The earth is whole and firm. The spirit is whole and full.

Returning is the motion of the Tao. Yielding is the way of the Tao. The 10,000 things are born of being. Being is born of nonbeing.

The weak overcomes the strong; the soft surpasses the hard. In all the world, there is no one who does not know this, but no one can master the practice.

The best governor

governs least.

The sage loves himself but does not exalt himself.

*Being content
with what you
have is always
best in the end.*

Someone must risk

returning injury with

kindness or hostility

will never turn

to goodwill.

*One with true
virtue always seeks
a way to give. One
who lacks true
virtue always seeks
a way to get.*

The sage prefers

what is within

to what is without.

The master is pointed

but does not pierce;

he straightens but

does not disrupt;

he illuminates but

does not dazzle.

*True words are
not beautiful;
beautiful words
are not true.*

Remember:

A tree that fills a man's

embrace grows from a seedling.

A tower nine stories high

starts with one brick.

A journey of a thousand miles

begins with a single step.

Good men do not argue; those who argue are not good.

*Should you want
to eliminate something,
you must deliberately
allow it to flourish.*

*Sages do not accumulate
anything but give everything
to others; having more,
the more they give.*

Do not resist the natural

course of your life.

In this way you will never

weary of this world.

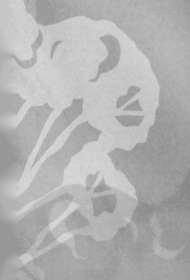

If you overvalue

possessions,

people begin

to steal.

*By not displaying what is
desirable, you will
cause people's hearts
to remain undisturbed.*

The Tao seems

to be the common

ancestor of all,

the father of things.

The sage stays

a witness

to life, so he

endures.

Govern with equity.

Be timely in choosing

the right moment.

The sage acts for

the people's benefit;

he trusts them;

he leaves them

alone.

Working, yet not taking

credit; leading without

controlling or dominating.

One who heeds this power

brings the Tao to this very earth.

*The master allows
things to come
and go. He prefers
what is within to
what is without.*

One who loves

himself as everyone

is fit to be teacher

of the world.

From mercy comes courage. From frugality comes generosity. From humility comes leadership.

*Although dark
and obscure, the
Tao is the spirit,
the essence, the life
breath of all things.*

To know

heaven,

understand

the Way.

*If you preserve
your original
qualities, you can
govern anything.*

Bragging . . .

showing off . . .

self-righteousness . . .

when walking the path of

the Tao, this is the very stuff

that must be uprooted, thrown

out, and left behind.

All people are

drawn to the sage.

He behaves like

a little child.

In this world,

the more artful and crafty

the plan, the stranger

the outcome; the more laws

are posted, the more

thieves appear.

The sage says:

"If I keep from imposing on people, they become themselves."

The female overcomes the male with stillness, by lowering herself through her quietness.

The Tao is the treasure

of the good man

and the refuge

of the bad.

Only when we

are sick

of our sickness

shall we cease

to be sick.

The sage helps the 10,000 things find their own nature but does not venture to lead them by the nose.

To the giver comes the fullness of life; to the taker, just an empty hand.

The master does not

think that he is better

than anyone else.

The wise always

give without

expecting

gratitude.

When a leader

trusts no one,

no one trusts him.

If you stand on tiptoe, you cannot stand firmly. If you take long steps, you cannot walk far.

For a knower of the truth,

the door he shuts,

though having no lock,

cannot be opened.

The knot he ties,

though using no cord,

cannot be undone.

When a sage stands

above the people, they do not

feel the heaviness of his

weight; and when he stands

in front of the people,

they do not

feel hurt.

*Be not moved
by attachment
or aversion, swayed by
profit or loss, or touched
by honor or disgrace.*

The supreme good

flows to low places

loathed by all men.

Therefore, it is

like the Tao.

One who lives in

accordance with nature

moves in harmony with

the present moment,

always knowing the truth

of just what to do.

To fulfill one's destiny

is to be constant.

To know the constant

is called insight.

How do you know

the ways of all things

at the beginning?

Look inside and see

what is within you.

*The successful
person, although
surrounded
by opulence,
is not swayed.*

There is a time for
being vigorous
and a time for being
exhausted; a time for
being safe and a
time for being
in danger.

The sage does not strive and yet attains completion.

If there is a good

store of virtue,

then nothing

is impossible.

The master remains

serene in the midst

of sorrow; evil cannot

enter his heart.

*Do not cast
the wicked man
away; cast away
his wickedness.*

The sage does

not treasure what

is difficult to attain.

To know the Way,

understand the great

within yourself.

The sage imitates
the ways of heaven,
acting for the
good of all and
opposing himself
to no one.

Within the Tao,

the sun is softened

by a cloud; the dust

settles into place.

*Heaven does
not hurry,
yet it completes
everything on time.*

Although the Tao

is invisible, it endures;

it will never end.

No matter how much

you use the Tao,

it cannot be exhausted.

In this world,

the more advanced

the weapons of state,

the darker the nation.

*When you adhere
to the Way, your
actions become
those of nature,
your ways those
of heaven.*

The brittle is easily shattered; the small is easily scattered.

Serene. Empty.

Solitary. Unchanging.

Infinite. Eternally

present. This is

the Tao.

Stuffing oneself with food and drink, amassing wealth to the extent of not knowing what to do with it . . . this is not the Tao.

The sage sees everything as his own self; he loves everyone as his own child.

You need not

fear darkness

when the light is

shining everywhere.

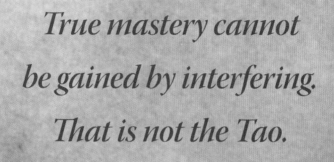

*True mastery cannot
be gained by interfering.
That is not the Tao.*

Heaven does
good to all,
doing no evil
to anyone.

Acknowledgments

I thank the translators and
authors of the following ten books:

*The Essential Tao: An Initiation into the Heart
of Taoism through the Authentic Tao Te Ching
and the Inner Teachings of Chuang Tzu,*
translated and presented by Thomas Cleary

*The Illustrated Tao Te Ching: A New Translation
with Commentary,* by Stephen Hodge

Tao Te Ching, by Lao Tsu;
translated by Gia-Fu Feng and Jane English

Tao Te Ching: The Definitive Edition, by Lao Tzu;
translation and commentary by Jonathan Star

Tao Te Ching: A New English Version,
by Stephen Mitchell

Tao Te Ching, by Lao Tzu; translated by John C. H. Wu

Tao-Te-Ching: A New Translation, by Lao-Tzu; translated by Derek Bryce and Léon Wieger

Tao Te Ching: A New Translation, by Lao Tzu; translated by Sam Hamill

A Warrior Blends with Life: A Modern Tao, by Michael LaTorra

The Way of Life According to Lao Tzu, translated by Witter Bynner

About the Author

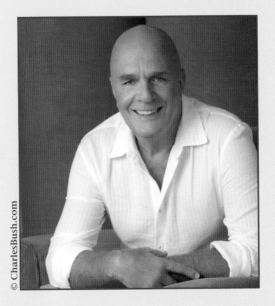

Dr. Wayne W. Dyer is an internationally renowned author and speaker in the field of self-development. He's the author of numerous books, has created many audio programs and videos, and has appeared on thousands of television and radio shows. His books *Manifest Your Destiny, Wisdom of the Ages, There's a Spiritual Solution to Every Problem,* and *The New York Times* bestsellers *10 Secrets for Success and Inner Peace, The Power of Intention, Inspiration, Change Your Thoughts—Change Your Life,* and *Excuses Begone!* have all been featured as National Public Television specials.

Wayne holds a doctorate in educational counseling from Wayne State University and was an associate professor at St. John's University in New York.

Website: **www.DrWayneDyer.com**

***

Notes

Notes

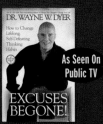

Hay House Titles of Related Interest

Healing Words from the Angels, by Doreen Virtue

Manifest Your Desires, by Esther and Jerry Hicks
(The Teachings of Abraham®)

Never Mind Success . . . Go for Greatness! by Tavis Smiley

101 Ways to Jump-Start Your Intuition, by John Holland

The Present Moment, by Louise L. Hay

The Secrets of Life, by Stuart Wilde

Secrets of the Lost Mode of Prayer, by Gregg Braden

Squeeze the Day, by Loretta LaRoche

Vitamins for the Soul, by Sonia Choquette

All of the above are available at your local bookstore, or may be ordered through the contact info on the next page.

We hope you enjoyed this Hay House Lifestyles book. If you'd like
to receive our online catalog featuring additional information
on Hay House books and products, or if you'd like to find
out more about the Hay Foundation, please contact:

Hay House, Inc.
P.O. Box 5100
Carlsbad, CA 92018-5100

(760) 431-7695 or **(800) 654-5126**
(760) 431-6948 (fax) or **(800) 650-5115 (fax)**
www.hayhouse.com® • **www.hayfoundation.org**

Published and distributed in Australia by: Hay House Australia
Pty. Ltd., 18/36 Ralph St., Alexandria NSW 2015 • *Phone:*
612-9669-4299 • *Fax:* 612-9669-4144 • www.hayhouse.com.au

Published and distributed in the United Kingdom by: Hay House
UK, Ltd., 292B Kensal Rd., London W10 5BE • *Phone:*
44-20-8962-1230 • *Fax:* 44-20-8962-1239 • www.hayhouse.co.uk

Published and distributed in the Republic of South Africa by:
Hay House SA (Pty), Ltd., P.O. Box 990, Witkoppen 2068
Phone/Fax: 27-11-467-8904 • info@hayhouse.co.za
www.hayhouse.co.za

Published in India by: Hay House Publishers India, Muskaan
Complex, Plot No. 3, B-2, Vasant Kunj, New Delhi 110 070 • *Phone:*
91-11-4176-1620 *Fax:* 91-11-4176-1630 • www.hayhouse.co.in

Distributed in Canada by: Raincoast, 9050 Shaughnessy St.,
Vancouver, B.C. V6P 6E5 • *Phone:* (604) 323-7100
Fax: (604) 323-2600 • www.raincoast.com

Take Your Soul on a Vacation

Visit **www.HealYourLife.com**® to regroup,
recharge, and reconnect with your own magnificence.
Featuring blogs, mind-body-spirit news, and
life-changing wisdom from Louise Hay and friends.

Visit **www.HealYourLife.com** today!

In dwelling, be close to the land. In meditation, go deep in the heart.

The Tao is the most

noble thing in the world.